The Blueprint to R.   ~~~~~   Pi 3

A Beginners Guide:
Everything You Need to Know for
Starting Your Own Projects

By: CyberPunk Architects

2

Introduction

Thank you for downloading my book *"Raspberry Pi: The Blueprint for Raspberry Pi 3: Everything You Need to Know for Starting Your Own Projects"*. Recently the Raspberry Pi has been receiving a ton of press coverage and capturing the curiosity of people all around the world, at least people who are technology journalists and enthusiasts. As time has passed, more and more people have heard of this fascinating small single board computer stamped with chips and connectors, but many people aren't sure exactly what it is.

If you are one of those people who is intrigued by the tastily named Raspberry Pi, this book is for you. In this book, we are going to look at a quick overview of what the Raspberry Pi is, and then we are going to break down the specifications and what they mean. Finally, we are going to look at all the amazing projects the Raspberry Pi can assist you with. Whether you are well-versed in technology or diving into it for the first time, this book is going to help you.

By the time, you are done reading this book, you are going to have the knowledge to use your Raspberry Pi with ease to do anything from watching a movie to playing games, and from creating a spreadsheet to learning how to program.

Chapter 1: Raspberry Pi – An Overview

The Raspberry Pi has many incredible features. The largest appeal of the Raspberry Pi computer is that it is a small size, and is also affordable. The Raspberry Pi can be used as a traditional computer by simply being plugged into a TV and a keyboard. Since 2012, there have been many models of the Raspberry Pi released to the public, each with their own improvements and changes.

Approximately the size of a credit card and available for as little as $5USD, the intended purpose of the Raspberry Pi was to bring affordable computer options to everyone. Below, we are going to take a brief look at the different models of Raspberry Pi.

Raspberry Pi 1 Model A – This was the original model of the Raspberry Pi. Released in February 2012. This was followed up late by the Raspberry Pi 1 Model A Plus which was released in November 2014, which featured a larger hard drive and a lower price point.

Raspberry Pi 1 Model B– The Generation 1 and 1 Plus of the Model B Raspberry Pi were released in April 2012 and July 2014 respectively. The 1 Plus had a lower price point than the original Model B and featured a microSD slot instead of the standard SD slot.

Raspberry Pi Zero – This was a smaller model that was released in November 2015. The size of the Zero was smaller and it had a reduced input and output. This is the cheapest model of Raspberry Pi that is currently available for purchase. The original Zero did not include video input. However, a second version released in May 2016 included video input options similar to other models.

Raspberry Pi 2 – This model included more ram than any of the previous models and was released in February 2015. This model is at the high end of all Raspberry Pi products and can be found for just $35USD.

Raspberry Pi 3 Model B – This is the newest model of Raspberry Pi. Released in February 2016, the Raspberry Pi 3, Model B is bundled with the additions including onboard Wi-Fi, Bluetooth, and USB boot capabilities. We will cover more on this later in this book.

There are a few things that are common among all the versions of Raspberry Pi. This includes the Broadcom system on a chip, which features a CPU (Central Processing System) that is compatible with ARM, as well as on-chip GPU (Graphics Processing Unit).

The boards all have between one and four USB slots, as well as an HDMI slot, composite video output and a 3.5 mm phone jack for audio capabilities.

The creators of Raspberry Pi provide *Raspbian*, which is a Debian-based Linux distribution for download. It also provides third party *Ubuntu, Windows 10* IOT Core, RISC OS, and other specialized media center distributions. While the Raspberry Pi supports many programming languages, it promotes Python and Scratch as its main programming language. You also have the option of open source or closed source firmware, although the default firmware is closed source.

Chapter 2: Raspberry Pi 3 – Model B Hardware Specifications

There have been several evolutions in the hardware that the Raspberry Pi offers. In this chapter, we are going to focus on the Raspberry Pi 3 – Model B specifically.

For the purpose of keeping this book easy to read for those of you who aren't as familiar with the technological jargon, while keeping it interesting for those of you who don't need as in depth of an explanation, this chapter is going to be broken down into sections that allow you to skim through and find the information you are looking for without having to read every explanation.

Wireless Radio – Broadcom BCM43438

This wireless radio has been expertly built directly into the board to keep the cost of the Raspberry Pi down. It is also so small; you are going to be able to see the markings through a microscope or magnifying glass. The Broadcom BCM43438 chip gives the Raspberry Pi 2.4 GHZ 802.11n wireless LAN, Bluetooth Low Energy, and Bluetooth 4.1 Classic radio support. This is what is going to allow you to connect your Raspberry Pi to the internet, both through a wired connection as well as through a wireless connection.

SoC – Broadcom BCM2837

This SoC (System on Chip) has been built specifically for the

Raspberry Pi 3 – Model B. This SoC features four high-performance ARM Cortex-A53 processing cores which run at 1.2GHz and have 32kB level one and 512kB level two memory. It also has a Video Core IV graphics processor and is also linked to the one gigabyte LPDDR2 memory module that is located on the rear of the board.

GPIO – 40-Pin Header, Populated

The GPIO (General Purpose Input Output) header is the same on this Raspberry Pi as it has been going back through most of the Raspberry Pi models. This means that any existing GPIO hardware is going to work with the Raspberry Pi 3 – Model B without any further modifications needed. The only change that has been made to this part of the Raspberry Pi is a change to which UART is exposed on the pins. However, this doesn't affect usage as the operating system internally handles it.

USB Chip – SMSC LAN9514

This is another part of the Raspberry Pi that hasn't changed from the Raspberry Pi 2. The SMSC LAN9514 adds 10/100 Ethernet connectivity as well as four USB channels to the board. The chip connects to the SoC through a single USB channel, acting as a USB to Ethernet adaptor as well as a USB hub.

To sum up all the information above:

SoC: Broadcom BCM2837

CPU: 4× ARM Cortex-A53, 1.2GHz

GPU: Broadcom VideoCore IV

RAM: 1GB LPDDR2 (900 MHz)

Networking: 10/100 Ethernet, 2.4GHz 802.11n wireless

Bluetooth: Bluetooth 4.1 Classic, Bluetooth Low Energy

Storage: microSD

GPIO: 40-pin header, populated

Ports: HDMI, 3.5mm analog audio-video jack, 4× USB 2.0, Ethernet, Camera Serial Interface (CSI), Display Serial Interface (DSI)

Now that we are all familiar with the hardware that is inside the Raspberry Pi 3 – Model B, we are going to have a look at the software.

Chapter 3: Raspberry Pi 3 – Software Specifications

One of the neat things about the Raspberry Pi 3 – Model B is that you can run almost any software on it. While it primarily uses *Raspbian*, which is a Debian-based Linux operating system, you are not limited to using this. In this chapter, we are going to run through all the different operating systems, driver APIs, firmware and other third party application software that will be accessible to you for use on the Raspberry Pi 3 – Model B.

Operating Systems

On the official Raspberry Pi website, you will have access to Ubuntu Mate, Snappy Ubuntu Core, Windows 10 IoT Core, and RISC OS, as well as specialized distributions for the Kodi media center and classroom management. Below we are going to cover every operating system that can be used, categorized by those that are Linux based and those that not Linux based.

Linux Based Operating Systems:

Alpine Linux – This is a Linux distribution that is based on *musl* and *BusyBox*. It has been primarily designed for those power users who require more security, simplicity, and resource efficiency.

Android Things – This is an embedded version of the Android operating system that is designed for IoT device development.

Ark OS – This operating system has been designed for website and email self-hosting.

CentOS – This is a newer operating system that is only available for Raspberry Pi 2 and newer.

Diet Pi – This operating system includes a diverse range of servers that are ideal for media, Minecraft, VPN, and much more.

Fedora 25 – This is another newer operating system that is only available for the newer Raspberry Pi models.

Gentoo – This operating system is ideal for users who want full control of the software that they use on their Raspberry Pi 3.

Instant WebKiosk – This operating system is ideal for users who are looking for digital signage purposes such as web and media views.

Kali Linux – This operating system is a Debian derived distro that has been designed for digital forensics and penetration testing.

Kano OS – This operating system is one that you can build and customize to be exactly what you want it to be for you. Completely free, this is a great choice if you want to have full control over your operating system.

MinePeon – This operating system has been designed to be dedicated to mining cryptocurrency.

Moebius – This is another operating system that is based on Debian. This operating system is a light ARM HF distribution that uses Raspbian repository but fits onto a 128 MB SD card. This operating system only offers minimal services and has had its memory use optimized to keep it small.

NARD SDK – This is a software development kids that is intended for industrial embedded systems.

OpenSUSE – This is another operating system that gives you full control over creating the code for your system.

OpenWrt – This operating system is primarily used to route network traffic on embedded devices.

Pardus ARM – This operating system is another option for a Debian derived system. This is the light version of the Pardus operating system that is popular with the Turkish Government.

Pidora – This is a Fedora Remix that has been optimized for use on the Raspberry Pi.

ROKOS – This operating system is another Rasbian based option that is integrated for use with Bitcoin and OKCash cryptocurrencies.

Tingbot OS – This operating system has been designed to be used primarily with the Tingbot add-on as well as running Tide applications. This operating system is also based on the Raspbian operating system.

Tiny Core Linux – This operating system is designed to run primarily in RAM. It is a minimal Linux operating system where the primary focus is to provide a base system using BusyBox and FLTK.

Void Linux – This operating system is a rolling release Linux distribution that has been designed and implemented from scratch. Void Linux provides images based on musl or glibc.

WTware for Raspberry Pi – This is a free operating system that is used for the creation of Windows thin client.

Xbian – This operating system uses the Kodi open source digital media center.

Not Linux Based Operating Systems:

Genode OS Framework – This operating system is a toolkit that is used to build highly secure special purpose operating systems. This is not the operating system that would be best for those who are just starting out, however, if you have a lot of experience with coding, this is a good choice.

HelenOS – This operating system is a portable multi-server that is microkernel-based.

NetBSD – This operating system is another that will allow you to create the coding and use your Raspberry Pi 3 – Model B however, you decide.

Plan 9 – This is an open source operating system that is similar to Unix. It was originally developed at Bell Labs as a research operating system. When you are using Plan 9, everything is treated as a file regardless of whether it is a local or network resource.

Xv6 – This is a modern version of the Sixth Edition Unix operating system that has been re-implemented for teaching purposes. It is easily ported to the Raspberry Pi from MIT xv6 which can be booted from NOOBS (New Out of Box Software).

Media Center Operating Systems – If you are looking for operating systems that are going to run your Raspberry Pi 3 – Model B as a media center your best options are OSMC, OpenELEC, LibreELEC, XBIAN, and Rasplex.

Audio Operating Systems – If you want to use your Raspberry Pi 3 – Model B for audio, the best operating systems are going to include Volumio, Pimusicbox, Runeaudio, and moOdeaudio.

Retrogaming Operating Systems – If you want to use your Raspberry Pi 3 – Model B to play retro games, the ideal operating systems include Retropie, Recalbox, Happi Game Centre, Lakka, ChameleonPi, and Piplay.

Driver APIs

Raspberry Pi 3 – Model B has the capability to use a VideoCore IV GPU through a binary blob. The binary blob is loaded into the GPU when it is booted from the SD card. Much of the driver work was originally done using the closed source GPU code, although there are software applications such as OpenMAX, OpenGL ES, or OpenVG which can be used to call an open course driver in the VideoCore IV GPU driver code.

Firmware

The official firmware of the Raspberry Pi 3 – Model B is a closed course binary blob that is freely redistributable. There is also open source firmware that is available minimally.

Third Party Application Software

As well as the operating systems that we covered in this chapter, there are many options for other software that can be put onto your Raspberry Pi 3 – Model B from third parties. In this section, we are going to briefly look at some of the more popular third party applications.

Mathematica – Raspbian includes a full installation of this software for free. This allows programs to be run from either a command line interface or from a notebook interface. Some of the language functions allow for accessing connected devices.

Minecraft – In February 2013, a version of Minecraft was released for Raspberry Pi that allows you to modify the game world with code. This is the only official version of Minecraft that allows this.

RealVNC – RealVNC's remote access server and viewer software are included with the Raspbian operating system. This includes the new capture technology which allows content to be directly rendered as well as non-X11 applications to be viewed and controlled remotely.

UserGate Web Filter – In 2013, Entensys, a security vendor based in Florida, announced they would be porting Usergate Web Filter to the Raspberry Pi Platform.

Software Development

In addition to the addition applications listed above, there are programs available that can help you learn more about developing software. Learning how to develop software will help you be able to use the Raspberry Pi 3 – Model B to its fullest potential.

AlgolD – This is a program that is ideal for teaching programming to children as well as beginners in the programming world.

Julia – This is a programming language that is both interactive and able to be used across multiple platforms. IDE's for Julia are also available including June and JuliaBerry, which is a Pi specific repository.

Scratch – This teaching tool uses visual blocks that stack to teach IDE. MIT's Life Long Kindergarten group originally developed this. The version that was created for Pi is heavily optimized for the limited computing resources that are available and work well with the Squeak Smalltalk system.

Now that you are aware of the software options that are available for you to use with your Raspberry Pi 3 – Model B, we are going to explore how you can go about configuring your Raspberry Pi to do what you want it to do.

Chapter 4: Configuring Raspberry Pi

Once you have your Raspberry Pi 3 – Model B in your possession, you are going to want to get it set up and ready to use. The good news is that setting it up is easy and takes less than thirty minutes. That means that before you know it, you are going to be ready to start doing some awesome stuff with your new piece of technology!

Before You Start

Before you get started, there are a few supplies you are going to need on hand in addition to the Raspberry Pi to get through the set-up process and move on to amazing projects.

HDMI television or monitor – You are going to need to connect your Raspberry Pi to a display which means that you need some sort of HDMI enabled screen. You don't need to use a full-sized monitor for your Raspberry Pi, and there are compact options on the market. There are also ways around using a monitor at all, which we will discuss later in this chapter.

USB keyboard and mouse – In order to be able to control your Raspberry Pi 3 – Model B, you are going to need to have a keyboard and mouse. Any USB keyboard and mouse will work for this.

8GB MicroSD card and card reader – Instead of using a hard drive, Raspberry Pi's operating system is installed with a MicroSD card. You are going to want at least 8Gb for this. Your computer might have a card reader. If it does not, all you are going to need is a cheap one,. Card readers can often be found for under $10 USD.

Power Supply – The Raspberry Pi 3 – Model B is powered by a micro USB, similar to the one you likely use for your cell phone. Since the Pi 3 – Model B has four USB ports, the best power supply is one that can provide at least 2.5A of power.

Step One – Install Raspbian Onto Your MicroSD Card with NOOBs

The first thing you are going to have to do before you can use your new Raspberry Pi 3 – Model B is to put Raspbian onto your MicroSD card. To do this, you first need to download the operating system on another computer and transfer it to your SD card. There are two ways you can do this. First, you can install Raspian manually. This required you to either know the command line, or external software. The second option, which is much simpler requires that you download and install NOOBs Since this is the easier option, this is the option we are going to review in this chapter.

1 – Put your SD card into your computer or SD card reader.

2 – Download NOOBs. Choose the option of "offline and network install." This option will include Raspbian in the download itself.

3 – You may need to format your SD card as FAT. If so, download the SD Association's Formatting Tool which can be found at sdcard.org. Simply set the "Format Size Adjustment" to "on" in the options menu, and your SD card will be formatted.

4 – Extract the Zip file. Once the extraction is complete, copy the entire folder contents to your SD card. Once the copy is complete, you can eject your SD card and insert it into your Raspberry Pi 3 – Model B.

Step Two – Hook Up Your Raspberry Pi

The next step is to connect your devices to your Raspberry Pi 3 – Model B. Doing this is very easy, since all you need to do is plug stuff into the USB ports. However, it is important to do this is in the order listed below to ensure that all of your devices are recognized when you boot your Raspberry Pi up.

1 – Connect your monitor to your Raspberry Pi

2 – Connect your USB mouse and keyboard

3 – If you are using an Ethernet cable for your router, connect it now.

4 – Connect your power adapter. Since your Raspberry Pi 3 – Model B doesn't have a power switch, as soon as you connect the power source it is going to turn on.

Step Three – Set Up Raspbian

When you first boot up NOOBs, it is going to be busy for a couple of minutes formatting the SD card and setting things up. Let it do what it needs to do. Eventually, there will be a screen that will come up asking you to install an operating system.

1 – At the bottom of the screen there is going to be a place where you can select your language and keyboard layout for your region.

2 – Check the box that is next to the Raspbian option and click install.

NOOBs will then run the installation process, which can take anywhere from ten to twenty minutes. Once it is complete, the Raspberry Pi will restart itself and then send you straight to the Raspbian desktop where you will have the ability to configure everything else.

Step Four – Configure Your Raspberry Pi 3 – Model B

Your Raspberry Pi is now mostly ready to go. In Raspbian you are going to see a start menu. In this start menu, you are going to be able to select applications, open a file browser, and execute other commands that you might expect to be able to do with an operating system. The first thing you should do is set up your Wi-Fi, as well as any Bluetooth devices you want to use, with your Raspberry Pi.

Connect to Your Wi-Fi Network

Connecting to Wi-Fi through your Raspbian is just as easy as any modern operating system you may be accustomed to working with.

1 – Click the network icon. It is located at the top right corner and looks like two computers.

2 – Select your Wi-Fi network name and enter your password.

That's it. You are now connected to your Wi-Fi network. You are only going to need to do this once, and it will work in both the command line and the graphical interface.

Connect Bluetooth Devices

If you want to use a Bluetooth enabled mouse or keyboard with your Raspberry Pi 3 – Model B, you are going to need to pair them. Depending on the device you are pairing, this process can vary a bit, but using the directions below, you shouldn't have any issues.

1 – Click on the Bluetooth icon that is in the upper right corner of your screen.

2 – Click the "Add Device" option

3 – Find the device that you want to pair your Raspberry Pi with and follow the directions that appear on the screen to pair them up.

Once you have followed the directions above, your Raspberry Pi 3

– Model B is ready for you to start playing around with. If something goes wrong and you end up somehow messing up the programming, you can also follow the above steps to reinstall Raspbian and start over.

Connect to Your Raspberry Pi Remotely

Occasionally you might find yourself in a position where you may want to access your Raspberry Pi remotely. Maybe you don't have access to a monitor, or you only have a laptop in the house. Whatever reason you may have for wanting to connect remotely, it's handy to know that there are options.

Connect to The Command Line Through SSH – You can use SSH from any computer to connect to the command line interface of your Raspberry Pi. While this option won't allow you to access a graphic interface, you can run any type of command from the Terminal application, and it'll execute on the Raspberry Pi. This is especially useful if you are working on a project that doesn't require a screen.

Use VNC To Use Your Home Computer as A Remote Screen – If your project requires that you do have a graphical interface, VNC (virtual network computing) to obtain it. You will be able to see the Raspberry Pi's desktop in a window on your computer desktop, and you will be able to control it like you are using the Pi. This isn't the best option for the day to day use as it is slow, but in the event that you only need to get a few things established and don't want to necessarily have to use the keyboard and mouse, this is an easy way to do so.

Now that you know how to get your Raspberry Pi 3 – Model B up and running, in the next chapter, we are going to look at some of the programming associated with your Raspberry Pi.

Chapter 5: Programming In Raspberry Pi

The original purpose of the Raspberry Pi was to be able to teach people about technology. In this chapter, we are going to learn some of the basics of the two programming languages that are included in Raspbian, which is the recommended distribution for the Pi.

Scratch

This is a great language for those who are learning the basics of programming. Scratch doesn't require you to get the text perfect. Instead, everything is done by dragging and dropping program blocks into your script. This also means that you aren't going to have to remember any of the commands. For this example, we are going create a simple drawing program that will allow us to use the arrow keys to trace lines on the screen.

The first thing you are going to have to do is open Scratch. You will find Scratch in the **Menu**, under **Programming**. Once you have opened Scratch, you will see a screen with blocks of code, a scripts area, a stage where you can see your project, as well as some toolbars.

Now that we have the program open, we are going to create the code that will let us move the cat sprite around the screen.

We are going to use three separate blocks, each of which will be executed when a key is pressed. First, press the yellow control button, which is located on the left side of the screen near the top. Drag and drop the option "**When Space Key Pressed**" into the scripts box. This is going to create a script that will run whenever the space key is pressed. Use the drop-down menu and change **Space** to **Right Arrow**. Click on the blue motion button that is located next to the yellow control button and drag **Move 8 Steps** under **Right Arrow** in the scripts window. This will allow you to move the cat forward by pressing the right arrow.

Now that you have done that, create similar scripts that turn clockwise when the down key is pressed, and counter clockwise when the up key is pressed. Once you have finished that, we will be able to move around. However, we will need to add a block that will allow us to draw. Since we don't want to draw all the time, we will use Scratch's **pen up** and **pen down** actions. When the pen is down, the cat will leave a line behind it. When the pen is up, the catwon't.

In order to toggle between having the pen up and the pen down, we are going to require the code to remember which state the pen is in. Programs use variables to do this. A variable is a chunk of memory that allows you to place data in and read data from. Before you are going to be able to use a variable, you are going to have to tell the computer to assign memory to it. We are also going to assign it a name that we can use to refer to it in the commands.

Go to **Variables,** in the same area you found control and motion, click on **Make a Variable,** and give it the name **Pen**. Once you have done this, you are going to see a selection of commands that are able to alter or use the variable. Now that we have a way to store the date, we are going to tell the computer to change its

24

behavior based on what the variable is. This is done using an **If...
Else** block. This is going to ask if a statement is true. If it is, it will execute the first block of code. If not, it will execute the second.

In our program, we are going to take the variable, **Pen**. If it is 0, we are going to put the pen down, then set it to one. Otherwise, we will lift the pen and set it to be 0. In this way, we are going to be able to toggle between the two states by using the spacebar.

Now you can move the cat around and draw a picture. However, wouldn't it be even better if you could insert a predefined item? We are going to learn how to add circles next. Technically it is going to be a twenty-four-sided shape, but it will look similar to a circle.

The method to do this is to **move forward 10**, then **rotate 15 degrees**, then **move forward 10**, then **rotate 15 degrees**, and keep doing this until you have completed the circle, which would require you to put in the same two lines twenty-four times. This would work, but it isn't the best way. Not only would it look terrible in the coding and be time consuming, but if you wanted to change the size of the circle, you would need to do this twenty-four times. The good news is, there is a better option.

Instead of writing out the code twenty-four times, can instead use a loop. A loop is a block that repeats itself. There are different types of loops, some that will keep going until a statement becomes false, and some that execute a set number of times. For this, we are going to use one that executes a set number of times.

You can find the loop option in the yellow control tab. We are going to use just two commands: **move forward 10**, and **rotate 15 degrees.** We will then set this to happen twenty-four times.

Now that you know how to use Scratch, you can play around with Scratch and discover just how much you can do with this programming software. (Peers, 2015)

Python

While Scratch is great to help you to learn the basics of programming, sooner or later you are going to reach its limitations and want to move onto something new. Python is a popular general-purpose programming language that is also easy to learn.

The first thing you need to be aware of is that Python is entirely text-based. This doesn't mean that it is unable to create graphics, but rather that your program code is going to written text instead of the drag and drop blocks we used in Scratch.

Before you get started with Python, it is important to know that since Python is text-based, you can use any text editor to create your programs. Leafpad comes with Pi and is a great starting point. Avoid using word processors such as LibreOffice Writer as they mess up the formatting and won't allow your program to function correctly.

First, open the Pi **menu** and choose **Programming** and then **Python 3**. This is the command line, but since we want to access IDLE's text editor, we are going to choose **File** and **New** to create a new blank document. On the first line type:

#!/usr/bin/python

This line is going to tell the system to use the program python, in the folder /usr/bin/ to run the file. This is important to add to the start of all the programs you create with Python.

In the programming world, there is a long-standing tradition of having your first program output "Hello World!" and we aren't going to break it here! Leave the second line blank and on the third line type:

Print "Hello World!"

26

Save your work in a file called hello.py.

Skipping a line in your coding is not strictly necessary. However, it makes your code easier to read.

To run the program we just created, open a terminal and navigate to where you saved the file. The default will be your home folder. First, type the following command to tell the system the file is executable:

$ chmod a+x hello.py

Next, type this command to run your program:

$ ./hello.py

You should see Hello World! appear on the screen. This shows us that the system is running properly. However, this program is not a very useful program.

(Peers, 2015)

Like we did with Scratch, we are going to add some user input. With the Python program, we are going to need to add a variable to store what the user types are. Delete the line with Hello World, leaving the top line, and add the line:

Name = raw_input('what is your name')

This line is going to create the variable name, display the prompt, "what is your name?", and store what the user types are. We must place this in inverted commas so the computer can recognize it as a single chunk of text. We are then going to be able to use this variable to make our print statement a little more personal with the line:

print 'Hello', name

Since the computer is going to run the commands in order, this one needs to be below the previous one. If you were to reverse the order they are in, the computer will register an error because we are trying to use a variable before we have even created it. You can now save the file and enter **./hello.py** at the command line to run the program.

This makes the program more functional, but leaves it relatively lifeless. In order to make it more useful, we need to add a step where the computer must look at what was inputted and perform a different task based on that input. If you recall the **If** block in Scratch, we are going to do something similar here except, we are actually going to write the code. The basic structure is going to be:

if :

code block

This must be replaced with something that can be true or false. In our case, we are going to check if the name entered is a particular value:

If name == 'Jane' :

Why ==? Computers don't deal well with ambiguity. Every symbol or word that we use can only have one meaning. Otherwise, things start to get confusing. The equal sign, "=", is used to assign a value to a variable, so we need to use something else to check the equality. Again, we are going to enclose **Jane** in inverted commas so the computer can recognize it's text. The colon tells the computer that we have finished our expression, and we are about to tell it what to do.

We may want this **If** command to run through more than one line of code. This means that we need a way to group code into blocks. This is done using indents in Python. Indents can be either a space or a tab. However, it is crucial to use the same method throughout your project to avoid confusion. Python doesn't read the amount of indentation, but rather the number of indents you have made.

Personally, I use two spaces for each indent, because that's how I was taught, and it makes it simple to keep it all the same.

Back to our programming. Now we want the computer to do something **if name == 'Jane'** so we have to tell the computer what we want it to do.

if name == 'Jane' :

 print "Jane, you're awesome"

Note that there are two spaces at the start of the second line. There are also double speech marks. This is because the text we have enclosed has an apostrophe in it. Since we don't want to be rude to all the people who aren't Jane, we are going to add an else block that runs whenever the above expression is false:

else :

 print 'hello', name

One last feature we are going to include is a loop. This is going to work similar to the one we created in Scratch, except it isn't going to only run twenty-four times. Instead, it will run until we tell it to stop. We are going to do this using a while look and the syntax:

while :

code block

We can have the program stop by entering the **name quit**. This means our **while** loop will be:

while name !: 'quit' :

For some reason, exclamation marks are often used to mean "not in the programming world". However, we are still left with a bit of a problem. If we put it before **name = raw_input...** we are going to produce an error because the computer doesn't know what **name** is. But if we put it after, it will only ask us to enter a name once, then spit the greeting out indefinitely, which is also not ideal.

There is a way to solve this. We are simply going to string the name before **while**. This stops the error and will always trigger the **while** expression. So, the program should look like this:

```
#!/usr/bin/python

name = "

while name != 'quit' :
name = raw_input('What is your name?')

if name == 'Jane' :
    print "Jane, you're awesome"
else :
    print 'Hello', name
```

You should note that there are four spaces before each print line. This is because they have been indented twice. Once for the **while** loop and once for the **if** statement. Now you can save this as hello.py and as before, run it with ./hello.py.

Both Scratch and Python are great programs to get started with, so now you can pick the one that appealed to you the most. In the next chapter, we are going to look at some sample project ideas that you can use to get started with programming your Raspberry Pi 3 – Model B.

Chapter 6: Sample Project Ideas For Your Raspberry Pi

Now you know all the technical information about your Raspberry Pi 3 – Model B, as well as some of the basics about using it for programming. From here we are going to go over some sample projects you can do, or build off of, as you begin to learn all that your Raspberry Pi can do.

<u>Turn Your Raspberry Pi into A Wireless Access Point</u>
There are many different reasons you might want to turn your Raspberry Pi into a wireless access point. Here are some of the most common reasons:
- Extend your existing Wi-Fi Network;
- Learn more about wireless networking;
- Create a free Access Point;
- Build a honey trap to learn about network hardening;
- Learn about sniffing packets;
- Provide guest wireless access that is firewalled through your main network;
- Closed Wi-Fi monitoring station for weather recording, temperature sensing; and
- Create a Raspberry Pi Hot Spot.

The first thing you need to do is ensure that your Raspberry Pi 3 – Model B is all set up and ready to be used. Assuming that it is, you are now going to run **sudo raspi-config** and set up your Pi, changing your memory split to sixteen. You are then going to reboot and set a password, if you choose to, for the root user. Assuming that you are logged in under Root User, you are now going to install Aptitude with **apt-get install aptitude**. Once this is installed, you are going to use the command **aptitude update; aptitude safe-upgrade**. The speed of your internet is what will determine how long this process is going to take.

Once that has finished, you are going to install a few packages:

Aptitude install rfkill zd1211-firmware hostapd-utils iw dnsmasq

These are:

rfkill – Wireless utility

zd1211-firmware – Software for dealing with zd1211 based wireless hardware

hostapd – This is the hostap wireless access point

hostap-utils – These are the tools that go with hostap

iw – Wireless configuration utility

dnsmasq – A DHCP and DNS utility

An addition option is to add **vim** to that list. Vim is a nicer console editor than the default vi.

Next, you are going to locate the file /etc/dhcpcd.conf. Once you have found this file, you are going to add these lines to the end:

interface wlan0

static ip_address=192.168.1.1/24

static routers=192.168.0.1

static domain_name_servers=8.8.8.8 8.8.4.4

These lines are going to instruct dhcpcd to statically configure the WLANO interface with an IP address. You can change this IP address to whatever you are intending to use for your wireless network. However, you must leave the /24 as it is important and the coding will not work without it. At this time, you should change the gateway from the default 192.168.0.1 to whatever the gateway is on your normal LAN which the wired ETHO interface is connected to. Leave the domain_name_servers as is, that's the Google DNS farm and should always work.

The next thing we are going to do is configure hostap. We are going to edit /etc/hostapd/hostapd.conf to look like this:

interface=wlan0

driver=nl80211

ssid=test

channel=1

Ensure that you don't leave any spaces at the end of each line, as hostap is very literal in reading its configuration and spaces will alter how the language is being read.

Finally, you are going to configure dnsmasq to allow yourself to obtain an IP address from your new Pi Point. Edit /etc/dnsmasq.conf to look like this:

 # Never forward plain names (without a dot or domain part)

domain-needed

 # Only listen for DHCP on wlan0

interface=wlan0

 # create a domain if you want, comment it out otherwise

#domain=Pi-Point.co.uk

 # Create a dhcp range on your /24 wlan0 network with 12

hour lease time
dhcp-range=192.168.1.5,192.168.1.254,255.255.255.0,12h

 # Send an empty WPAD option. This may be REQUIRED to get windows 7 to behave.
#dhcp-option=252,"\n"

Remember that you are going to change the dhcp-range to match the network IP address you are using. To ensure that your Pi Point is going to work after it is rebooted, you are going to need to create a run file that will turn on forwarding, nat and run hostap at the time of booting. To do this you are going to create a file named /etc/init.d/pipoint with the following contents:

#!/bin/sh
 # Configure Wifi Access Point.
#
BEGIN INIT INFO
 # Provides: WifiAP
 # Required-Start: $remote_fs $syslog $time
 # Required-Stop: $remote_fs $syslog $time
 # Should-Start: $network $named slapd autofs ypbind nscd nslcd
 # Should-Stop: $network $named slapd autofs ypbind nscd nslcd
 # Default-Start: 2
 # Default-Stop:
 # Short-Description: Wifi Access Point configuration
 # Description: Sets forwarding, starts hostap, enables NAT in iptables
END INIT INFO
 # turn on forwarding

```
echo 1 > /proc/sys/net/ipv4/ip_forward
# enable NAT
iptables -t nat -A POSTROUTING -j MASQUERADE
# start the access point
hostapd -B /etc/hostapd/hostapd.conf
```

Next make the script executable with **chmod +x /etc/init.d/pipoint** and add the script to the startup sequence of the Raspberry Pi using **update-rc.d pipoint start 99 2**. This will ensure that your Pi Point will reboot itself as a functioning Wi-Fi access point.

Turn Your Raspberry Pi 3 – Model B Into A Retro Arcade Machine

Who doesn't love retro video games? This project is going to show you how to very simply turn your Raspberry Pi into a retro games console in no time.

First, open up a terminal window. You can find this at the top of the screen. Once it's open, type **sudo apt-get update** followed by **sudo apt-get install -y git dialog**. Next, you are going to type **cd** and then **git clone git://github.com/petrockblog/RetroPie-Setup.git**. This is going to download a little script that is going to install tons of game emulators for you. To prepare the installer, type: **cd RetroPie-Setup**, then **chmod +x retropie_setup.sh**.

In the same terminal window, we are going to type: **sudo./retropie_setup.sh**, this is going to run the installer and bring up an awesome retro interface. Once we are here, we are going to select the binaries-based install option. This is going to take about an hour.

Once this is installed, we are going to open up another terminal window and type: **sudo raspi-config**. In this configuration app, you are going to go into the boot options and choose to make the Pi boot into a command prompt instead of Raspbian. Now you are going to reset the Pi, and then type **EmulationStation** to run your new retro game center.

This is going to give you access to emulators for more than twenty systems, including the Mega Drive and Nintendo 64. While some games are going to be built in, you are going to have to check out a site like *emuparadise.*

Create A Media Center With Your Raspberry Pi

Before you get started on making your Raspberry Pi into a media center, you are going to need to obtain a few components:

- Raspberry Pi Case
- Standard SD card
- Micro-USB cable and wall charger
- HDMI cable
- USB mouse and keyboard

The first thing you are going to do is get your Raspberry Pi set up in the case. The board should fit snugly in the case without needing to be forced in. Once you have placed your Raspberry Pi into your case and screwed the top on, you are ready to move on.

The media center is going to run on RaspBMC Linux distribution, and you are going to need to download this from a computer other than the Raspberry Pi. Once you unzip the file, right click the file **setup.exe** and select "Run as Administrator" click yes to the User Account Control dialog. You will then be presented with an interface which will allow you to install the RaspBMC to an SD card. Next, select the SD card from the list and check the box stating that you agree with the license agreement and select install.

Now that the software has been installed on the SD card, you are going to insert it into the Raspberry Pi. Turn the Raspberry Pi on and begin the installation process. This can take up to forty-five minutes.

Now that RaspBMC has been installed, you are going to be given the option to choose a language, and will then be greeted with the home screen. Scroll over to the program section and select the RaspBMC settings option. This is going to allow you to change your connection type from wired to wireless. You are going to be able to change many other settings to personalize your experience. Now you are ready to add your media. Since it is impractical to store your media on the SD card, we are going to be streaming the media from an existing computer.

Go to the home menu and navigate to the video option. Here, you should see a drop-down option for files, choose this option and then click the option to add videos. This should give you a menu that allows you to browse for a source.

Select browse. A screen will appear that contains a variety of options to connect. XBMC facilitates a number of different connection options. However, most computers are going to rely on the Windows Samba option, which you will find near the bottom. Once you have clicked on this option, it is going to ask you for the username and password for the computer you are trying to stream from. Enter this information, and you will be able to view the files that you have chosen to share. Now that you have added your media, you should be able to select the media and begin streaming content.

There are three different methods you can use to control the device you have just created.

1 – A wireless mouse is one option, although it is also the most

inconvenient.

2 – There are various apps you can get for your Android or iPhone.

3 – A universal remote. This is the most ideal option since you likely already have one of these in your home.

There are many, many more things you can do with your new Raspberry Pi 3 – Model B. We've walked through two of the most popular, and easiest, things you can do. Below is a list of other things that your Raspberry Pi is capable of. Feel free to attempt any of these projects, or create one of your very own, the only limit with the Raspberry Pi is your imagination.

Other Raspberry Pi Projects
- Write your own game
- Make a Gameboy (advanced)
- Make a Kodi streamer
- Build a download hub
- Create a dedicated Minecraft machine
- Build a camera trap
- Build a case for your Raspberry Pi
- Control your stereo wirelessly
- Create your own cloud server
- Make a phone
- Make a PiRate radio station
- Build a smart beer fridge
- Make a PiCam
- Make a talking toy
- Make a bitcoin mining machine
- Create a tiny arcade
- Build your own virtual assistant, similar to Amazon's Alexa

- Build a Raspberry Pi laptop

- Stream PC games to the Pi

- Raspberry Pi music player

- Raspberry Pi photo frame

- Make a motion sensor

- Raspberry Pi security camera network

- Build a Samba server

- Create a smart mirror

As you can see, the options of what you can do with the Raspberry Pi are virtually endless. Choose a project to get started with, and remember, if something ever goes wrong, simply go back to the beginning and reprogram your Raspberry Pi as if it were brand new.

Chapter 7: Accessories For Your Raspberry Pi 3 – Model B

Costing only $35, the Raspberry Pi is a great price, and it also very basic. However, there are many accessories you can get for your Raspberry Pi if you want to spend the money. In this chapter, we are going to briefly look at some of the available accessories and the pros and cons of each one. We are also going to take a look at what you would get from each accessory, whether that be aesthetic, functionality or something else.

Raspberry Pi 3 Starter/Media Center Kit – For anyone who is buying the Pi 3, particularly if it is the first Pi owned, a starter kit can be a huge benefit. It comes with a power supply, a case, an 8GB micro SD card, HDMI and Ethernet cables. It also includes NOOBs, Raspbian, and Kodi pre-installed.

HDMI to VGA Adapter – HDMI is very common. However, it's still not everywhere. If you have a monitor that is not HDMI enabled, or you just prefer VGA, this is one attachment that will make your life a lot easier.

Raspberry Pi Heatsink – The Raspberry Pi 3 – Model B produces heat. If you are going to be doing advanced projects, it is going to produce more heat. To extend the life of the processor, a heatsink is a great option.

Raspberry Pi Touchscreen – Touchscreens are everywhere, and if you are planning on making a Pi Phone or tablet, this is a great product to have. While most of the touchscreens you are going to find are only 480p, it is still better than a non-touch display.

Camera Module – Almost every device available these days has a camera. Adding a camera to your Raspberry Pi will allow you to use it as a video calling box, home security system or even as an actual camera.

Pi Sense Hat – There are some things you probably never considered you might need. Like temperature sensors, humidity sensors and an LED sensor. The PiSense Hat also has an accelerometer, a magnetic sensor, a five-button joystick, and a barometer. This makes it an essential tool for many projects.

Adafruit RGB Matrix – If you are hoping to make a stunning light show, or just need a basic display to showcase things, this fully programmable color LED board is your ideal gadget.

Adafruit Perma Promo Hat – This is a basic tool that will allow you to create and test your own custom circuits for use in your projects.

PaPiRus eink Display Hat – This is perfect if you are looking for a basic display that isn't going to suck up a bunch of power. This display is great to display a calendar, clock, or thermometer.

<u>Mini Wireless Keyboard And Mouse Touchpad</u> – This is great if you don't want to keep your Pi connected to a mouse and keyboard all the time. You aren't going to want to use this when you are typing out long strands of commands. However, it is great if you are only typing a few sudo commands or small mouse movements.

<u>Cases</u> – There are many different cases you can get for your Raspberry Pi. From the simplest cases that are used just to protect your Raspberry Pi from the elements, to cases that include a touchscreen holder or even mount to a monitor.

As you can see, there are many different options for accessories for your Raspberry Pi. Most of the accessories you are going to find listed above are available for under one hundred dollars. This means that even if you choose to invest in a few of your favorites, you are still going to be spending less than you would be on a traditional computer, and you are going to be able to do so much more with it.

Conclusion

Now that you know the basics of the Raspberry Pi 3 – Model B, you are ready to venture out and start getting some hands-on experience with it. Remember, there is a ton of different software options that you can use when you are programming your Raspberry Pi, so you are by no means confined to the ones that came standard with the Raspbian that we downloaded in the walkthroughs.

Remember, the Raspberry Pi computers were created to give everyone an affordable option to learn about technology and how they can manipulate it. Use your imagination and enjoy the process of learning how to program your Raspberry Pi 3 – Model B to do virtually anything you want it to do.

I would like to thank you for downloading my book: *Raspberry Pi: The Blueprint for Raspberry Pi 3: Everything You Need to Know For Starting Your Own Projects*. I hope you found the content in this book to be a valuable contribution to what you are going to do with your Raspberry Pi.

Bibliography

Peers, B. E. (2015, December 29). Retrieved March 1, 2017, from http://www.techradar.com/news/software/learn-to-program-your-raspberry-pi-1148194